Seek & Hide

A Blackout Poetry ~~Work~~Play book

Jessica McHugh

Apokrupha Books

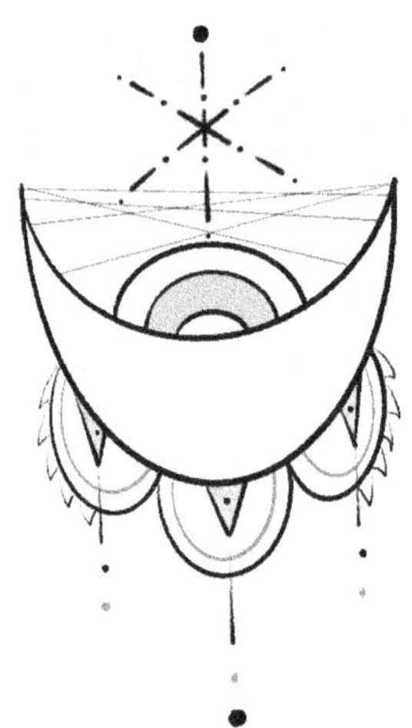

Cover and interior artwork by Jessica McHugh
mchughniverse.com

Cover design by Lynne Hansen
LynneHansenArt.com

Copyright 2024
Published by Apokrupha Books
apokrupha.com

Table of Contents

Publisher's Note   i

Who Are You, & What Are You Doing in My Room? 1

Lesson 1: Dropping Anchor   3

Lesson 2: In This Economy?   13

Lesson 3: Opposites Attract   39

Lesson 4: Alternate Routes   49

Lesson 5: This Is My Design   67

CHEAT CODES   85

Game On!   89

Jessica McHugh   101

Bibliography   102

Pen Test!   103

Apokrupha.com/Blackout

Download a PDF of pages to
print and play!

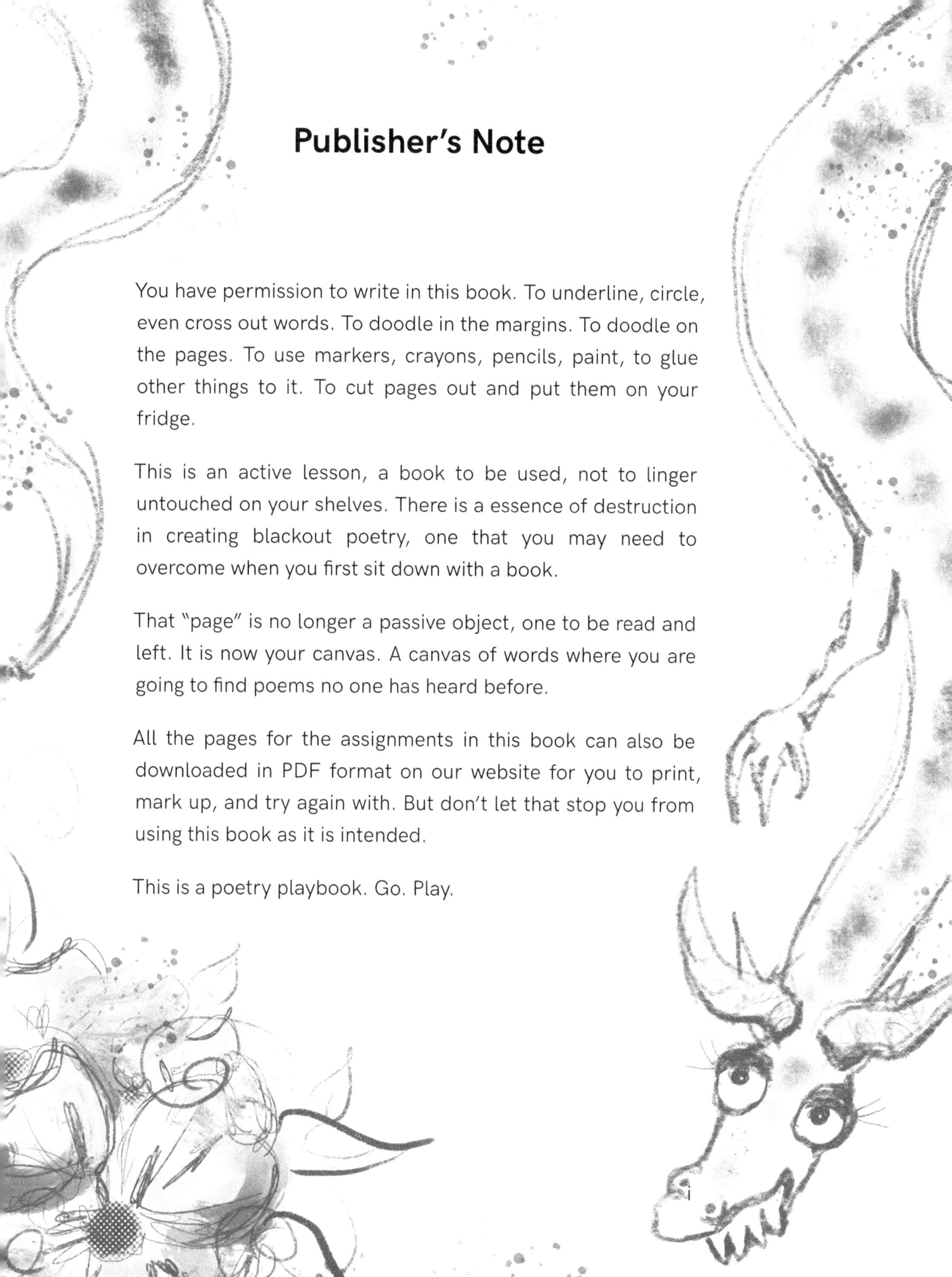

Publisher's Note

You have permission to write in this book. To underline, circle, even cross out words. To doodle in the margins. To doodle on the pages. To use markers, crayons, pencils, paint, to glue other things to it. To cut pages out and put them on your fridge.

This is an active lesson, a book to be used, not to linger untouched on your shelves. There is a essence of destruction in creating blackout poetry, one that you may need to overcome when you first sit down with a book.

That "page" is no longer a passive object, one to be read and left. It is now your canvas. A canvas of words where you are going to find poems no one has heard before.

All the pages for the assignments in this book can also be downloaded in PDF format on our website for you to print, mark up, and try again with. But don't let that stop you from using this book as it is intended.

This is a poetry playbook. Go. Play.

Who Are You, &
What Are You Doing in My Room?

Before we begin, I'd like to make one thing crystal clear. Yes, this is technically a "workbook," but I certainly don't want to be accused of making any of this seem like work. What follows will be more of a *PLAY* book, intended to educate new and seasoned writers about the stages and techniques of creating blackout poetry while provide a limitless space to explore creativity and expand the boundaries of poetic possibilities.

No counting syllables, no designated line structure to adhere to—though such effort is highly welcome and encouraged if that's your toast and jam. Hell, if you're able to finagle out a rhyming scheme, I tip my hat to you, but for the purposes of this playbook, we're going to take it easy and enjoy the ride. And the hunt, at times.

So, what is a blackout poem?

In the simplest terms, it's a poem you've found within an existing piece of text. More specifically, it's using a book page, a magazine article, a religious tract left on your windshield, etc. to write a poem by linking together select phrases, words, and letters. The term "blackout" refers the various art techniques you can use to cover up the superfluous words.

That art can be as simple as crossing out everything except the words of your poem, or as complex as using sculpture and papercraft to give the poem more dimension. Because of its many varietals, you might've heard of blackout poetry as one of its other names: erasure, redacted, found, collage poetry, or the cut-up technique.

With its use of pre-existing text, blackout poetry is the treasure hunter of the poetry world. It's the distiller, the refiner, the dumpster-diving scrapbooker of the poetry world. It's getting your hands dirty in pursuit of the perfect poem, weighing and measuring and learning the shapes of words, peering in and repurposing them, while either rebelling against or working in concert with the original text. You can let the words lead you or guide them down a path of your making because blackout poetry is a second and third and fourth chance for those words on that page to explore a different life.

Most of all, blackout poetry is whatever you want it to be.

Okay. Enough speeches. It's time for a rousing game of:

SEEK & HIDE.

Lesson 1:
Dropping Anchor

A finished page can be just as intimidating as a blank page. This is especially true when making blackout poetry because your blank page is a finished page. It's your task to treat it as both canvas and palette—and that's before we ever reach the artwork portion of the process—and create something new based on how you choose and use these words.

Of course, they carry all the weight of the book's original intent, as well as your personal connection to them, so part of the challenge of blackout poetry is viewing the page as if none of those influences exist. That's not to say your blackout piece can't use the original intent or even be a commentary on it—I'll give an example of this a little later—but it's often less pressure to divorce yourself from the meaning of the text.

I find it helps to view the page like a sea of random words. As you scan the page, some of these words and phrases will shine like buoys between the waves. Take note of these standouts, and consider if one (or more) might help you take the most important step of starting a blackout poem: finding your anchor.

Typically your anchor is the word or phrase that serves as the subject of your poem, but depending on the page, you might have a few solid choices. That's why it's important to pay attention to those buoy words. Take a swim, see what you're working with, and once you have an idea of where your poem's headed, go ahead and map things out.

Pencils are essential during the writing process. A drafting pencil that leaves light marks is best, as you might find yourself erasing a lot in pursuit of the perfect arrangement. How well the page handles this depends on the age, condition, and print quality. Some might take on a boatload of erasures with little effect, other might bear scars of experimentation after only one. Luckily, blackout poetry is a forgivable and adaptive medium that encourages the artist's creativity to cover the erroneous as well as the superfluous, something I'll expand on when we reach the design stage.

A Dip in the Like

If you're feeling timid about jumping in, try making a poem that starts with a simile or metaphor. Look for phrases like "I am…," "They are…", "Love's like…," and treat the rest like an artistic word search. This allows you room to explore the language set before you in new and interesting ways, as shown in the attached poem. This is something you can use to your advantage, leading the reader from a simplistic beginning, through a linguistic wilderness into a metaphor that becomes poignant, transformative, or a literary love letter like this piece created from William Shakespeare's MacBeth.

Enter Macbeth.

Great Glamis! worthy Cawdor!
Greater than both, by the all-hail hereafter!   60
Thy letters have transported me beyond
This ignorant present, and I feel now
The future in the instant.

Macbeth

Duncan comes here tonight.

Lady Macbeth

          And when goes hence?

Macbeth

Tomorrow, as he purposes.

Lady Macbeth

          O, never
Shall sun that morrow see!   70
Your face, my thane, is as a book where men
May read strange matters. To beguile the time,
Look like the time; bear welcome in your eye,
Your hand, your tongue: look like the innocent flower,
But be the serpent under't. He that's coming   75
Must be provided for; and you shall put
This night's great business into my dispatch;
Which shall to all our nights and days to come
Give solely sovereign sway and masterdom.

Macbeth

We will speak further.

Lady Macbeth

          Only look up clear;   80
To alter favor ever is to fear:
Leave all the rest to me.

          [*Exeunt.*

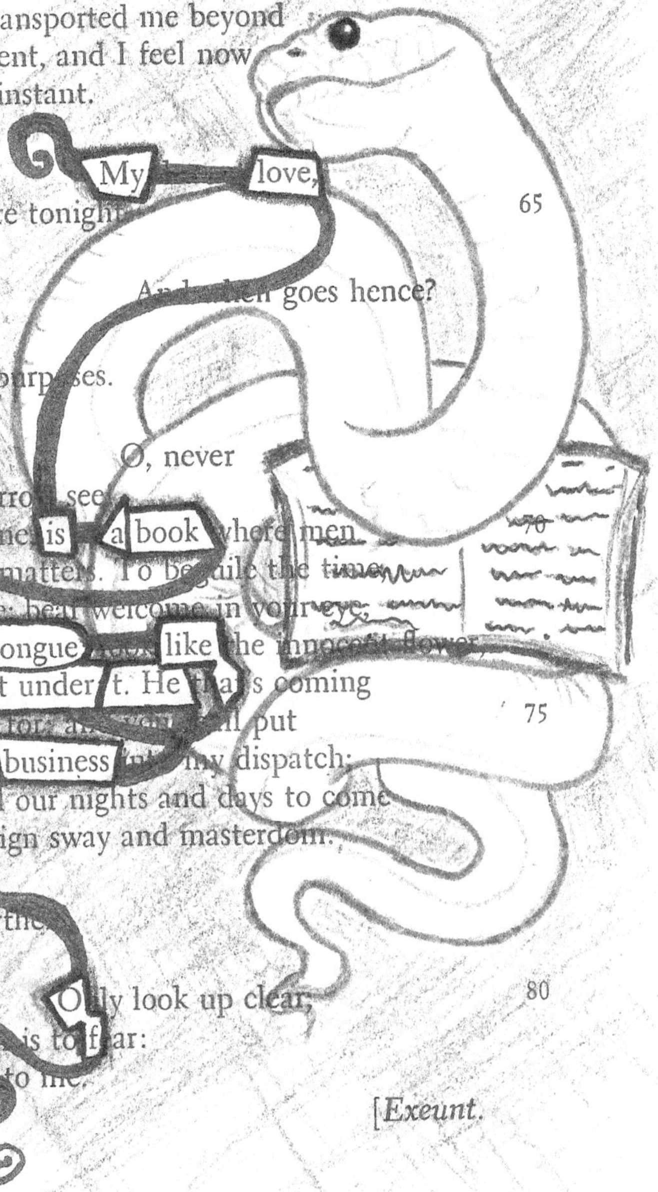

Nests

My love is a book:
A read tongue, like a serpent
Under the business of leaves

    —from Macbeth

Blackout Breakdown

What's a book? It's our read tongue, our language put to paper. But a book is also something that can consume us, playing with our thoughts and emotions. Much like love. Or...a wily serpent, with its red/read tongue darting. Love, books, serpents: all can inspire titillation, fear, dread, reverence, and delight, and they get down to business under various types of leaves. Snakes burrow in literal leaves, books are comprised of loose leaves (or sheets), and love's business often occurs under metaphorical leaves (also, sheets).

Wordplay can be your best friend when building a blackout poem, which we'll discuss further in Lesson 2. But first...

use the attached pages to make your own
poems starting with a metaphor or simile

'Why, kiss her awake, of course.'

'Not me!' was Gerald's unhesitating rejoinder.

'Well, someone's got to.'

'She'd go for me as likely as not the minute she woke up,' said Gerald anxiously.

'I'd do it like a shot,' said Kathleen, 'but I don't suppose it 'ud make any difference me kissing her.'

She did it; and it didn't. The Princess still lay in deep slumber.

'Then you must, Jimmy. I dare say you'll do. Jump back quickly before she can hit you?'

'She won't hit him, he's such a little chap,' said Gerald.

'Little yourself!' said Jimmy. '*I* don't mind kissing her. I'm not a coward, like Some People. Only if I do, I'm going to be the dauntless leader for the rest of the day.'

'No, look here—hold on!' cried Gerald, 'perhaps I'd better—' But, in the meantime, Jimmy had planted a loud, cheerful-sounding kiss on the Princess's pale cheek, and now the three stood breathless, awaiting the result.

And the result was that the Princess opened large, dark eyes, stretched out her arms, yawned a little, covering her mouth with a small brown hand, and said, quite plainly and distinctly, and without any room at all for mistake:

'Then the hundred years are over? How the yew hedges have grown! Which of you is my Prince that aroused me from my deep sleep of so many long years?'

'I did,' said Jimmy fearlessly, for she did not look as

—*from The Enchanted Castle*

that one little kiss whiles I bring over the table. Friend John, help to me!' So neither of us looked whilst he bent over her.

Van Helsing turning to me, said:—

'He is so young and strong and of blood so pure that we need not defibrinate it.'

Then with swiftness, but with absolute method, Van Helsing performed the operation. As the transfusion went on something like life seemed to come back to poor Lucy's cheeks, and through Arthur's growing pallor the joy of his face seemed absolutely to shine. After a bit I began to grow anxious, for the loss of blood was telling on Arthur, strong man as he was. It gave me an idea of what terrible strain Lucy's system must have undergone that what weakened Arthur only partially restored her. But the Professor's face was set, and he stood watch in hand and with his eyes fixed now on the patient and now on Arthur. I could hear my own heart beat. Presently he said in a soft voice: 'Do not stir an instant. It is enough. You attend him; I will look to her.' When all was over I could see how much Arthur was weakened. I dressed the wound and took his arm to bring him away, when Van Helsing spoke without turning round— the man seems to have eyes in the back of his head:—

'The brave lover, I think deserve another kiss, which he shall have presently. And as he had now finished his operation, he adjusted the pillow to the patient's head. As he did so the narrow black velvet band which she seems always to wear round her throat, buckled with an old diamond buckle which her lover had given her, was dragged a little up, and showed a red mark on her throat. Arthur did not notice it, but I could hear the deep hiss of indrawn breath which is one of Van Helsing's ways of betraying emotion. He said nothing at the moment, but turned to me, saying: 'Now take down our

–*from Dracula*

Lesson 2:
In This Economy?

You might've already heard and accepted the adage "Writing is rewriting," which refers to how much of the writing process actually occurs during the editing stage. If this is your first time hearing it, I apologize for being the bearer of bad news…and for expanding upon it by telling you math is also an integral part of the process. Writers don't need to be a professional editors, but it's beneficial to have an editor's awareness of word economy to make their piece as strong as possible, especially in short-form writing.

Word economy refers to the correlation between your writing's brevity and its strength. Channeling a "less is more" philosophy, it's the writer's challenge to use as few words as possible to convey their message without compromising the art or their voice. Like flash fiction, blackout poetry is a test in brevity…albeit with some more extreme vocabulary and space constraints. One of the biggest differences is the number of words at your disposal. Instead of working with the entirety of every language in existence, you only have what's on the page in front of you. It's not just about quantity, though.

Words have certain weights and values on their own. String them together, and those weights and values change. Switch them around, use them as double entendres, play with phonetics and semantics and polysyndetic rhythms, and you transform them into something else entirely.

An understanding of word economy also aids in long-form writing, so even if blackout and flash aren't your favorite art forms, experimenting with both can be beneficial elsewhere. You will never eliminate the editing process, nor should you try, but the more aware you are of word economy while writing, the stronger your first drafts can be.

Of course, there are some key differences between editing a story or poem you're writing from scratch, and one you're creating with blackout poetry techniques.

Rules Are Meant to be Broken

The constraints of tenses, points-of-view, and word orders can feel daunting, like you have no control beyond what the author provided. And you can stay true to that: use each full word, same tense, same order and directionality to create a fantastic piece. But you can break every rule too. You can split words, combine words, use individual letters to build words that span several lines, you can tack on "s" and "ed" to change tenses and use POVs that might not even exist in the original piece. As long as it's legible, you can do anything you want.

You're also working within someone else's vocabulary. For me, this is one of the most interesting parts of blackout poetry. Usually, one absorbs and sometimes adopts another writer's vocabulary through the act of reading, which is why it's essential to becoming a better writer. Reading immerses us in another artists' language and techniques more naturally than being sat down and instructed on the how-to of literature. But blackout poetry forces you to utilize another writer's vocabulary, like this deliciously evocative, ten-word poem created from Emily Bronte's *Wuthering Heights*:

than words could do, the intensest anguish at having made himself the instrument of thwarting his own revenge. Had it been dark, I dare say, he would have tried to remedy the mistake by smashing Hareton's skull on the steps; but, we witnessed his salvation; and I was presently below with my precious charge pressed to my heart.

Hindley descended more leisurely, sobered and abashed.

'It is your fault, Ellen,' he said, 'you should have kept him out of sight; you should have taken him from me! Is he injured anywhere?'

'Injured!' I cried angrily. 'If he's not killed, he'll be an idiot! Oh! I wonder his mother does not rise from her grave to see how you use him. You're worse than a heathen—treating your own flesh and blood in that manner!'

He attempted to touch the child, who, on finding himself with me, sobbed off his terror directly. At the first finger his father laid on him, however, he shrieked again louder than before, and struggled as if he would go into convulsions.

'You shall not meddle with him!' I continued, 'He hates you—they all hate you—that's the truth! A happy family you have; and a pretty state you're come to!'

'I shall come to a prettier, yet, Nelly,' laughed the misguided man, recovering his hardness. 'At present, convey yourself and him away—And, hark you, Heathcliff! clear you too, quite from my reach and hearing—I wouldn't murder you to-night, unless, perhaps, I set the house on fire: but that's as my fancy goes—'

While saying this he took a pint bottle of brandy from the dresser, and poured some into a tumbler.

'Nay, don't!' I entreated, 'Mr Hindley, do take warning. Have mercy on this unfortunate boy, if you care nothing for yourself!'

'Any one will do better for him than I shall,' he answered.

'Have mercy on your own soul!' I said, endeavouring to snatch the glass from his hand.

'Not I! on the contrary, I shall have great pleasure in sending it to perdition, to punish its maker,' exclaimed the blasphemer. 'Here's its hearty damnation!'

Walkthrough

My heart is a heathen
Slick as a murder-house.

> —*from Wuthering Heights*

I love the imagery this poem conjures, especially as it pertains to the similarities between a heart and a heathen, two things that can lose faith and / or be seen as corrupted and immoral, and a heart and a murder-house, both of which have blood-stained walls that could be described as "slick." But in true homophonic fashion, the word "slick" could also describe a smooth, shrewd heathen, which…aren't they all?

We'll go over design in more detail in Lesson 5, but I wanted to point out the reasoning behind this artwork. It could've gone a number of ways—I could've drawn a heart, maybe the flames of hell—but I chose to draw the murder-house specifically because of the shape created by the poem's word placement. It has a very structural flow, almost stacked, which lent itself well to a crooked, crumbling mansion. The windows and doors work well to help the chosen words stand out, I added the turret to corral the sprawling letters in "slick," and the broken shudder hanging off "murder" suggests the poem's direction, but also represents the hyphen in "murder-house."

Beggars Can Be Choosers

In the next section, I will break down how I weigh word option in a step-by-step example of writing the following poem:

Act As Though Awake

Grief has children that
stone the heart with Love

   —from Macbeth

Right away, "grief has children" jumped out at me. This is the anchor to which the rest of my poem will be tied. I included the word "that" in my anchor, but there were other options to explore.

Let's make us med'cines of our great revenge, 250
To cure this deadly grief.

Macduff

He has no children. All my pretty ones?
Did you say all? O hell-kite! All?
What, all my pretty chickens and their dam
At one fell swoop? 255

Malcolm

Dispute it like a man.

Macduff

　　　　　　　　　. I shall do so;
But I must also feel it as a man:
I cannot but remember such things were,
That were most precious to me. Did heaven look on, 260
And would not take their part? Sinful Macduff,
They were all struck for thee! naught that I am,
Not for their own demerits, but for mine,
Fell slaughter on their souls: heaven rest them now!

Malcolm

Be this the whetstone of your sword: let grief 265
Convert to anger; blunt not the heart, enrage it.

Macduff

O, I could play the woman with mine eyes,
And braggart with my tongue! But, gentle heavens,
Cut short all intermission; front to front
Bring thou this fiend of Scotland and myself; 270
Within my sword's length set him; if he 'scape,
Heaven forgive him too!

Malcolm

　　　　　　　　　This tune goes manly.
Come, go we to the king; our power is ready;
Our lack is nothing but our leave. Macbeth 275
Is ripe for shaking, and the pow'rs above
Put on their instruments. Receive what cheer you may;
The night is long that never finds the day.

　　　　　　　　　　　　　　　[*Exeunt.*

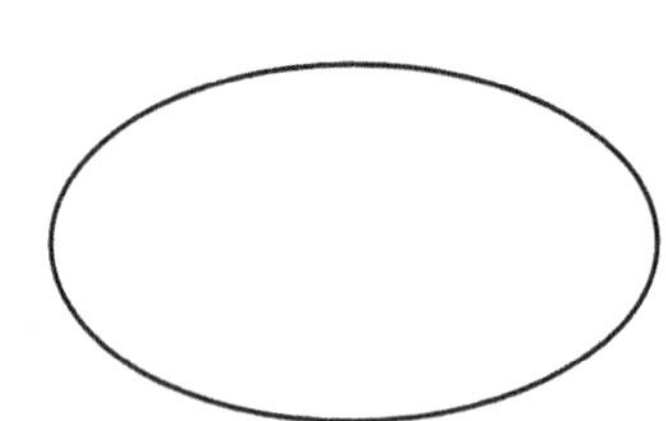

In scanning the page, these words stood out to me as a potential path from the initial phrase. They each inspire contrasting feelings and visuals. By the tenses, you can see I've decided to focus more on "children" from the anchor rather than "grief," as it invokes the stages and many complex effects of grief instead of the concept on its own. I would've also had to change the tenses if I'd focused on "grief." While it's not impossible to change tenses by adding s's, d's, etc, those letters aren't readily available on this page, and changing the words would overcomplicate the visual aspect of this piece.

"Slaughter" is probably the most evocative word of the group, but does it overpower the subject of the piece? That's definitely something I want to avoid. "Stone" is an interesting option because it has stirs up a few different images in me, notably feeling "hard as stone," and the act of throwing rocks at someone, like children skipping stones, but violently. That connection to children is a big plus. "Cut Short" is a great option because of death literally cuts short the lives of those we love. It also has a brilliant consonance with those t's at the end of each word.

Let's make us med'cines of our great revenge,   250
To cure this deadly grief.

Macduff

He has no children. All my pretty ones?
Did you say all? O hell-kite! All?
What, all my pretty chickens and their dam
At one fell swoop?   255

Malcolm

Dispute it like a man.

Macduff

                        I shall do so;
But I must also feel it as a man:
I cannot but remember such things were,
That were most precious to me. Did heaven look on,   260
And would not take their part? Sinful Macduff,
They were all struck for thee! naught that I am,
Not for their own demerits, but for mine,
Fell slaughter on their souls: heaven rest them now!

Malcolm

Be this the whetstone of your sword: let grief   265
Convert to anger; blunt not the heart, enrage it.

Macduff

O, I could play the woman with mine eyes,
And braggart with my tongue! But, gentle heavens,
Cut short all intermission; front to front
Bring thou this fiend of Scotland and myself;   270
Within my sword's length set him; if he 'scape,
Heaven forgive him too!

Malcolm

                        This tune goes manly.
Come, go we to the king; our power is ready;
Our lack is nothing but our leave. Macbeth   275
Is ripe for shaking, and the pow'rs above
Put on their instruments. Receive what cheer you may;
The night is long that never finds the day.

                                        [*Exeunt.*

( )

Verbs aren't the only words and phrases that stand out while scanning the page. With my anchor in mind, along with all those action words, I make note of imagery that also connects to "Grief has children." Words like "heart," "heaven," "love," and "night that never finds day" can all be molded into a piece about loss and help define what I'm trying to communicate to the reader about the subject.

Let's make us med'cines of our great revenge,　　　250
To cure this deadly grief.
Macduff
He has no children. All my pretty ones?
Did you say all? O hell-kite! All?
What, all my pretty chickens and their dam
At one fell swoop?　　　255
Malcolm
Dispute it like a man.
Macduff
　　　　　　　　· I shall do so;
But I must also feel it as a man:
I cannot but remember such things were,
That were most precious to me. Did heaven look on,　　　260
And would not take their part? Sinful Macduff,
They were all struck for thee! naught that I am,
Not for their own demerits, but for mine,
Fell slaughter on their souls: heaven rest them now!
Malcolm
Be this the whetstone of your sword: let grief　　　265
Convert to anger; blunt not the heart, enrage it.
Macduff
O, I could play the woman with mine eyes,
And braggart with my tongue! But, gentle heaven,
Cut short all intermission; front to front
Bring thou this fiend of Scotland and myself;　　　270
Within my sword's length set him; if he 'scape,
Heaven forgive him too!
Malcolm
　　　　　　　　This tune goes manly.
Come, go we to the king; our power is ready;
Our lack is nothing but our leave. Macbeth　　　275
Is ripe for shaking, and the pow'rs above
Put on their instruments. Receive what cheer you may;
The night is long that never finds the day.
　　　　　　　　　　　　[*Exeunt.*

As you start to make decisions and build your poem, you might need more linking, transition, and descriptive words, some of which I've highlighted here. The funny thing is, the words/phrases you notice last might become some of the most important of your piece, or even change the entire vibe. You just have to remain open to it and remember there isn't one correct answer to this puzzle. There are many answers, each uniquely beautiful and daring. It's up to you to choose the strongest words in the strongest configuration to best communicate the meaning of the piece.

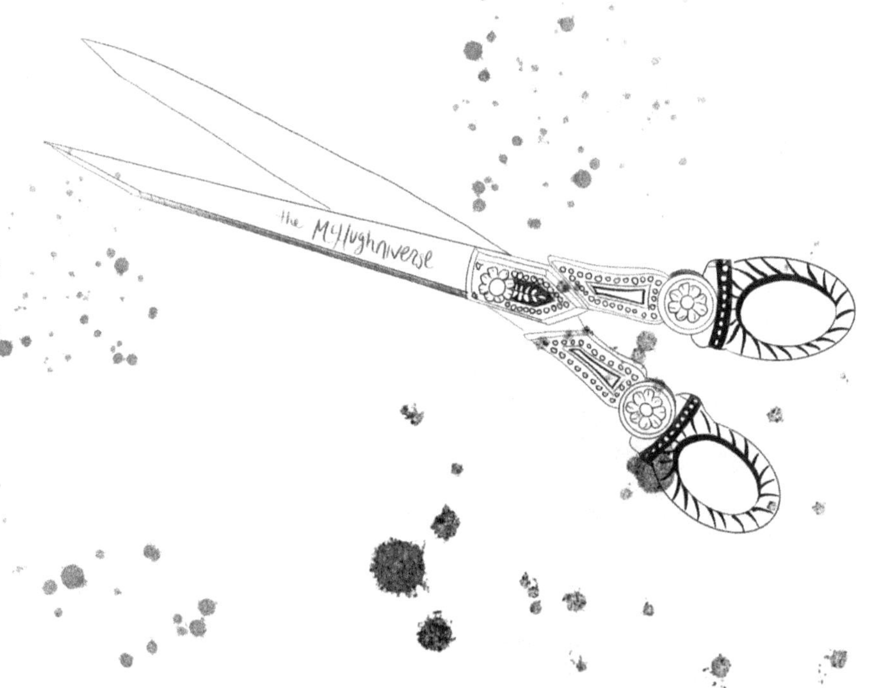

Let's make us med'cines of our great revenge,   250
To cure this deadly grief.
Macduff
He has no children. All my pretty ones?
Did you say all? O hell-kite! All?
What, all my pretty chickens and their dam
At one fell swoop?   255
Malcolm

Dispute it like a man.
Macduff

                    I shall do so;
But I must also feel it as a man:
I cannot but remember such things were,
That were most precious to me. Did heaven look on,   260
And would not take their part? Sinful Macduff,
They were all struck for thee! naught that I am,
Not for their own demerits, but for mine,
Fell slaughter on their souls: heaven rest them now!
Malcolm
Be this the whetstone of your sword: let grief   265
Convert to anger; blunt not the heart, enrage it.
Macduff
O, I could play the woman with mine eyes,
And braggart with my tongue! But, gentle heaven,
Cut short all intermission; front to front
Bring thou this fiend of Scotland and myself;   270
Within my sword's length set him; if he 'scape,
Heaven forgive him too!
Malcolm

                    This tune goes manly.
Come, go we to the king; our power is ready;
Our lack is nothing but our leave. Macbeth   275
Is ripe for shaking, and the pow'rs above
Put on their instruments. Receive what cheer you may;
The night is long that never finds the day.
                              [*Exeunt.*

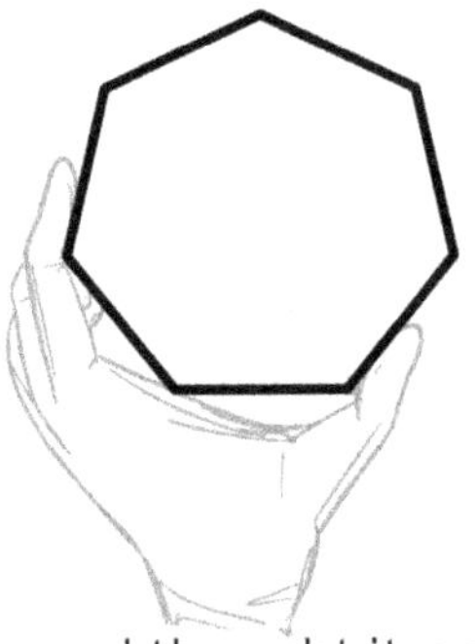

When I started this piece, I thought it would be morose, maybe even gory. But once I decided to focus on grief's children as the complex stages of mourning, I wanted to aim for a poem of tragedy and healing. The thought that we wouldn't grieve so hard if we hadn't loved so hard. I loved the imagery of children stoning someone paired with the thought of grief hardening their heart, for better or worse.

    Let's make us medicines of our great revenge,   250
    To cure this deadly grief.
Macduff
    He has no children. All my pretty ones?
    Did you say all? O hell-kite! All?
    What, all my pretty chickens and their dam
    At one fell swoop?   255
Malcolm

    Dispute it like a man.
Macduff

                    · I shall do so;
    But I must also feel it as a man:
    I cannot but remember such things were,
    That were most precious to me. Did heaven look on,   260
    And would not take their part? Sinful Macduff,
    They were all struck for thee! naught that I am,
    Not for their own demerits, but for mine,
    Fell slaughter on their souls: heaven rest them now!
Malcolm
    Be this the whetstone of your sword: let grief   265
    Convert to anger; blunt not the heart, enrage it.
Macduff
    O, I could play the woman with mine eyes,
    And braggart with my tongue! but, gentle heaven,
    Cut short all intermission; front to front
    Bring thou this fiend of Scotland and myself;   270
    Within my sword's length set him; if he 'scape,
    Heaven forgive him too!
Malcolm

                    This tune goes manly.
    Come, go we to the king; our power is ready;
    Our lack is nothing but our leave. Macbeth   275
    Is ripe for shaking, and the pow'rs above
    Put on their instruments. Receive what cheer you may;
    The night is long that never finds the day.
                                        [Exeunt.

A Little Fall of Rain

For this design, I wanted to channel the melancholy in the poem by using these circular vessels that both deflect and collect grief as it leaks into our lives. The last one accumulates it all, and at times it can feel like we're drowning in it, but in the end, the vessel of our lives is filled with so much grief because it's filled with so much love

Let's make us med'cines of our great revenge,   250
To cure this deadly grief.

Macduff

He has no children! All my pretty ones?
Did you say all? O hell-kite! All?
What, all my pretty chickens and their dam
At one fell swoop?   255

Malcolm

Dispute it like a man.

Macduff

                I shall do so;
But I must also feel it as a man:
I cannot but remember such things were,
That were most precious to me. Did heaven look on,   260
And would not take their part? Sinful Macduff,
They were all struck for thee! naught that I am,
Not for their own demerits, but for mine,
Fell slaughter on their souls: heaven rest them now!

Malcolm

Be this the whetstone of your sword: let grief   265
Convert to anger; blunt not the heart, enrage it.

Macduff

O, I could play the woman with mine eyes,
And braggart with my tongue! But, gentle heavens,
Cut short all intermission; front to front
Bring thou this fiend of Scotland and myself;   270
Within my sword's length set him; if he 'scape,
Heaven forgive him too!

Malcolm

                This tune goes manly.
Come, go we to the king; our power is ready;
Our lack is nothing but our leave. Macbeth   275
Is ripe for shaking, and the powers above
Put on their instruments. Receive what cheer you may;
The night is long that never finds the day.

                                        [Exeunt.

Flex your word economy muscles, and write a poem in ten words or less

'Well, yes, I do. I was learned that by a young lady I was gardener to. She had a lot in place she was fond of, an' she loved 'em like they was children—or robins. I've seen her bend over an' kiss 'em.' He dragged out another weed and scowled at it. 'That were as much as ten year' ago.'

'Where is she now?' Asked Mary, much interested.

'Heaven,' he answered, and drove his spade deeply into the soil, ''cording to what parson says.'

'What happened to the roses?' Mary asked again, more interested that ever.

'They was left to themselves.'

Mary was becoming quite excited.

'Did they quite die? Do roses die when they are left to themselves?' She ventured.

'Well, I'd got to like 'em—an' I liked her—an' she liked 'em,' Ben Weatherstaff admitted reluctantly. 'Once or twice a year I'd go an' work at 'em a bit—prune 'em an' dig around th' roots. They run wild, but they was in rich soil, so some of them lived.'

'When they have no leaves and look grey and brown and dry, how can you tell whether they are dead or alive?' inquired Mary.

'Wait till th' spring gets at 'em—wait till th' sun shines on th' rain an' the rain' falls on the sunshine an' then that'll find out.'

'How—how?' Cried Mary, forgetting to be careful.

'Look along th' twigs an' branches an' if tha' sees a bit of brown lump swelling here an' there, watch it after th' warm rain an' see what happens.' He stopped suddenly and looked curiously at her eager face. 'Why does the' care so much about roses an' such, all of a sudden?' He demanded.

Mistress Mary felt her face grow red. She was almost afraid to answer.

'I—I want to play that—that I have a garden of my own.' She stammered. 'I—there is nothing for me to do. I have nothing—and no one.'

'Well,' said Ben Weatherstaff slowly, as he watched her, 'that's true. Tha' hasn't.'

He said it in such an odd way that Mary wondered if he was actually a little sorry for her. She had never felt sorry for herself; she had only felt tired and cross, because she disliked people and things so much. But now the world seemed to be changing and getting nicer. If no one found out about the secret garden, she should enjoy herself always.

She stayed with him for ten or fifteen minutes longer and asked him as many questions as she dared. He answered every one of them in his

—*from Secret Garden*

and lock my door?"

She was lying with her tiny hands buried in her rich wavy hair, under her cheek, her little head upon the pillow, and her glittering eyes followed me wherever I moved, with a kind of shy smile that I could not decipher.

I bid her good night, and crept from the room with an uncomfortable sensation.

I often wondered whether our pretty guest ever said her prayers. I certainly had never seen her upon her knees. In the morning she never came down until long after our family prayers were over, and at night she never left the drawing room to attend our brief evening prayers in the hall.

If it had not been that it had casually come out in one of our careless talks that she had been baptised, I should have doubted her being a Christian. Religion was a subject on which I had never heard her speak a word. If I had known the world better, this particular neglect or antipathy would not have so much surprised me.

The precautions of nervous people are infectious, and persons of a like temperament are pretty sure, after a time, to imitate them. I had adopted Carmilla's habit of locking her bedroom door, having taken into my head all her whimsical alarms about midnight invaders and prowling assassins. I had also adopted her precaution of making a brief search through her room, to satisfy herself that no lurking assassin or robber was "ensconced."

These wise measures taken, I got into my bed and fell asleep. A light was burning in my room. This was an old habit, of very early date, and which nothing could have tempted me to dispense

—*from Carmilla*

Lesson 3:
Opposites Attract

It's a challenge exposing the drug-addled maniac hiding in the holiday classic, "The Night Before Christmas," or finding sunny rays of unburdened hope in "Where the Red Fern Grows," but there's also a fiendish sort of delight in creating a poem antithetical to its source material. You can make horror poems from Mother Goose and romantic poetry from splatterpunk. You can find science fiction in nonfiction and create bombastic comedies from historical dramas.

The Horrors Persist, But So Does Poetry

Despite the wide range of possibilities, I've found that dark and gory poems are the easiest to find in any genre of source material, due to the tendency for horror vocabulary to be evocative, onomatopoetic, and comfortable in many arenas of wordplay. From the sweetest words, one can write a poem like a shiv—sharp, deep, and so quick the reader might not even know they're reading a scary poem until you rip out the blade. A thoughtful design can amplify that, working in tandem with the poem to conjure feelings of anxiety, claustrophobia, or abyssal emptiness in a layered experience.

Once divorced from context, words become totems for our personal experiences and past contexts, intentionally or not. When building a found poem, you can choose to lean into those preconceived notions, or you can take a different path, reinterpret not only the direction of the road but the make of it as well. With that much freedom at your fingertips, you can twist a genre to your will, like the eldritch horror I discovered in a beloved children's fantasy novel.

The enchantment of the garden held him

'I'll not go in yet,' he told himself, 'it's too early. And perhaps I shall never be here at night again. I suppose it *is* the night that makes everything so different.'

Something white moved under the drooping willow; white hands parted the long, trailing branches and a figure came out, a creature with horns and goat's legs and the head and arms of a boy. And he was not afraid at all. Instead, a pleasant feeling, very rare in these latter days, a feeling that the world and he were one, warmed him through and through. He laughed. The creature leaped across the lawn, and something else came out from the willow; three steps nearer, and he saw that it was the pedestal of a statue—and it was empty.

'They're coming out,' he said, and another white shape came out from the temple of Flora and disappeared in the laurels. 'The statues come alive.'

There was a crunching of the little stones in the gravel of the drive. Something enormously long and darkly grey came crawling towards him, slowly, heavily. The moon came out just in time to show its shape. It was one of those great lizards that you see at the Crystal Palace, made in stone, of the same awful size which they were millions of years ago when they were masters of the world before Man was.

'It can't see me,' he said. 'I am dreaming. This has come to life too.'

As it writhed past him its vast body touched his side. He put his hand out. It was quite real. I had not 'come alive' as he had fancied. There was life in its stone. It lay there alive and breathing.

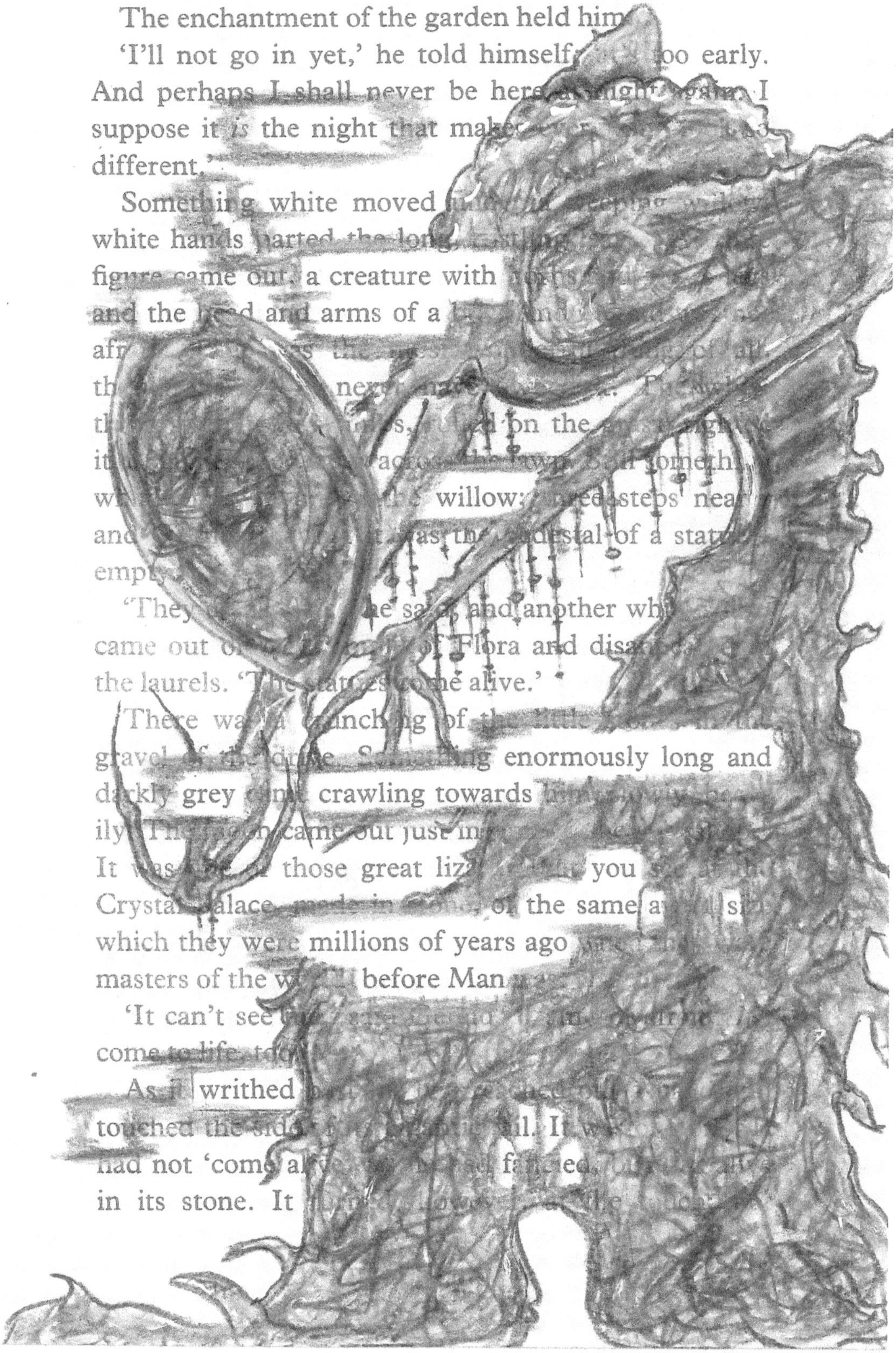

Shut the Door

The night is a creature
with the arms of a willow, enormously long and grey,
crawling towards you the same as millions of years ago,
before Man writhed to life.

—from The Enchanted Castle

With the phrase "The night is a creature," we set the scene for a scary time. But even after the addition of "with the arms of a willow," it's unclear whether the opening line is metaphorical or literal. Even after being described as "enormously long and grey" and "crawling towards you," it's up for debate whether the subject is an interpretation of night or an actual creature, but the accompanying artwork does imply that the night is a living thing hanging over then descending upon the world—and has been doing so since before humankind existed.

using the attached pages from the childhood classics
"The Secret Garden" & "The Enchanted Castle"
make your own spooky poems!

Chapter 6

'There was someone crying—there was!'

THE NEXT DAY THE rain poured down in torrents again, and when Mary looked out of her window the moor was almost hidden by grey mist and cloud. There.could be no going out today.

'What do you do in your cottage when it rains like this?' she asked Martha.

'Try to keep from under each other's feet mostly,' Martha answered. 'Eh. there does seem a lot of us then. Mother's a good-tempered woman, but she gets fair moithered. The biggest ones goes out in th' cow-shed and plays there. Dickon he doesn't mind th' wet. He goes out just th' same as if th' sun was shinin'. He says he sees things on rainy days as doesn't show when it's fair weather. He once found a little fox cub half drowned in its hole and he brought it home in th' bosom of his shirt to keep it warm. Its mother had been killed near by an' th' hole was swum out an' th' rest o' th' litter was dead. He's got it at home now. He found a half-drowned young crow another time an' he brought it home, too, an' tamed it. It's named Soot, because it's so black an' it hops an' flies about with him everywhere.'

The time had come when Mary had forgotten to resent Martha's familiar talk. She had even begun to find it interesting and to be sorry when she stopped or went away. The stories she had been told by her Ayah when she lived in India had been quite unlike those Martha had to tell about the moorland cottage which held fourteen people who lived in four little rooms and never had quite enough to eat. The children seemed to tumble about and amuse themselves like a litter of rough, good-natured collie puppies. Mary was most attracted by the mother and Dickon. When Martha told stories of what "mother' said or did they always sounded comfortable.

'If I had a raven or a fox cub I could play with it,' said Mary. 'But I have nothing.

Martha looked perplexed.

"Can tha' knit?' she asked.

—*from The Secret Garden*

scratched. As it was Mabel's hand was scraped between the cold rock and a passionate boot-heel. Nor will I tell you all that she said as they led her along the fern-bordered gully and through the arch into the wonderland of Italian scenery. She had but little language left when they removed her bandage under a weeping willow where a statue of Diana, bow in hand, stood poised on one toe, a most unsuitable attitude for archery, I have always thought.

'Now,' said Gerald, 'it's all over—nothing but niceness now and cake and things.'

'It's time we did have our tea,' said Jimmy. And it was.

Eliza, once convinced that her chest, though invisible, was not transparent, and that her companions could not by looking through it count how many buns she had eaten, made an excellent meal. So did the others. If you want really to enjoy your tea, have minced veal and potatoes and rice-pudding for dinner, with several hours of excitement to follow, and take your tea late.

The soft, cool green and grey of the garden were changing—the green grew golden, the shadows black, and the lake where the swans were mirrored upside down, under the Temple of Phoebus, was bathed in rosy light from the little fluffy clouds that lay opposite the sunset.
'It is pretty,' said Eliza, 'just like a picture-postcard, aint it? —the tuppenny kind.'

'I ought to be getting home,' said Mabel.

'I can't go home like this. I'd stay and be a savage and live in that white hut if it had any walls and doors,' said Eliza.

—*from The Enchanted Castle*

Lesson 4:
Alternate Routes

One page doesn't tell just one story. Nor does it always stay in one genre. Sometimes, one page contains multitudes. And as the treasure-hunting poet, you have the opportunity to explore every glittering trail. This page from MacBeth led me down two paths that start and move in relatively the same way. But while "Hot Drinks" is a romantic, even cheeky, poem spoken to another person, "Posset" has more of an self-empowering artistic vibe.

                                        [*Exit Servant.*

Is th... ...ne,
The ... ...me, let me clutch
    thee.
I have thee, ... yet I see thee still.

To feeling as to sight? or art ... But   45
A dagger of the mind, a false ...ion,
Proceeding from the heat-oppres... ...rain?
I see thee yet, in form as palpabl...
As this which now I draw.
Th... was going;   50
...ch an instrument I was to use.
...ine... are made the fools o' the other senses,
Or else...
And on thy blade and dudgeon gouts o...
Which was not so before. There's no such thing   55
It is the bloody business which informs
Thus to mine eyes. Now o'er the one half world
Nature seems dead, and wicked dreams abuse
The curtain'd sleep; witchcraft celebrates
Pale Hecate's offerings; and wither'd murder,   60
Alarum'd by his sentinel, the wolf,
Whose howl's his watch, thus with his stealthy pace,
With Tarquin's ravishing strides, towards his design
Moves like a ghost. Thou sure and firm-set earth,
Hear not my steps, which way they walk, for fear   65
Thy very stones prate of my whereabout,
And take the present horror from the time,
Which now suits with it. Whiles I threat, he lives:
Words to the heat of deeds too cold breath gives.
                                        [*A bell rings.*

I go, and it is done: the bell invites me.   70
Hear it not, Duncan, for it is a knell
That summons thee to heaven, or to hell.
                                        [*Exit.*

Hot Drinks

Let me clutch thee.
To feel thy form, nature and dream curtained in ravishing design,
I, firm-set for thy heat, live in heaven.

—*from Macbeth*

[*Exit Servant.*

Is this a dagger which I see before me,
The handle toward my hand? Come, let me clutch
    thee.
I have thee not, and yet I see thee still.
Art thou not, fatal vision, sensible
    To feeling as to sight? or art thou but   45
A dagger of the mind, a false creation,
Proceeding from the heat-oppressed brain?
I see thee yet, in form as palpable
As this which now I draw.
Thou marshal'st me the way that I was going;   50
And such an instrument I was to use.
Mine eyes are made the fools o' the other senses,
Or else worth all the rest. I see thee still,
And on thy blade and dudgeon gouts of blood,
Which was not so before. There's no such thing: 55
It is the bloody business which informs
Thus to mine eyes. Now o'er the one half-world
Nature seems dead, and wicked dreams abuse
The curtain'd sleep; witchcraft celebrates
Pale Hecate's offerings; and wither'd murder,   60
Alarum'd by his sentinel, the wolf,
Whose howl's his watch, thus with his stealthy pace,
With Tarquin's ravishing strides, towards his
Moves like a ghost. Thou sure and firm-set earth,
Hear not my steps, which way they walk, for fear 65
Thy very stones prate of my whereabout,
And take the present horror from the time,
Which now suits with it. Whiles I threat, he
Words to the heat of deeds too cold breath gives.
                                    [*A bell rings.*

I go, and it is done; the bell invites me.   70
Hear it not, Duncan; for it is a knell
That summons thee to heaven or to hell.
                                    [*Exit.*

Posset

Be a dagger for art
Fatal
Sensible
&
Worth the blood

—*from Macbeth*

Choose Your Own Adventure

With so many angles and avenues to explore, why let standard directionality constrain your creativity? In blackout poetry, there are no rules about starting and ending points or how the poem should flow. However, it's good to keep in mind that people are going to gravitate to their natural starting point, like the top left in written English. But while exploration is highly encouraged, legibility should be maintained, or at least controlled through the design, and if the poem doesn't have a traditional starting point, it's important to use the artwork to clarify where that poem begins.

For example, I've made two poems from Page 49 of Frankenstein, the first of which starts at the bottom. With vocabulary like "geography" and compass," this poem conjured map imagery for me, which I incorporated into the design. With the last line of the poem being "spot," using a large "X" to mark the end of the piece seemed appropriate. To make the starting point even clearer, I included a tiny paper sailboat indicating the beginning of our journey.

The second poem also has a sea travel feel, but without needing a special indicator to steer the reader, I used a simple, soft outline and obscured the superfluous text with a series of cresting waves.

the spot. The sky became clouded, but the air was pure, although chilled by the northeast breeze that was then rising. But it refreshed me and filled me with such agreeable sensations that I resolved to prolong my stay on the water, and fixing the rudder in a direct position, stretched myself at the bottom of the boat. Clouds hid the moon, everything was obscure, and I heard only the sound of the boat as its keel cut through the waves; the murmur lulled me, and in a short time I slept soundly.

I do not know how long I remained in this situation, but when I awoke I found that the sun had already mounted considerably. The wind was high, and the waves continually threatened the safety of my little skiff. I found that the wind was northeast and must have driven me far from the coast from which I had embarked. I endeavoured to change my course but quickly found that if I again made the attempt the boat would be instantly filled with water.

Thus situated, my only resource was to drive before the wind. I confess that I felt a few sensations of terror. I had no compass with me and was so slenderly acquainted with the geography of this part of the world that the sun was of little benefit to me. I might be driven into the wide Atlantic and feel all the tortures of starvation or be swallowed up in the immeasurable waters that roared and buffeted around me. I had already been out many hours and felt the torment of a burning thirst, a prelude to my other sufferings. I looked on the heavens, which were covered by clouds that flew before the wind, only to be replaced by others; I looked upon the sea: it was to be my grave. 'Fiend,' I exclaimed, 'your task is already fulfilled!' I

Unexpected Vessel

Your task is to look around this geography with no compass
And lull everything to an agreeable spot.

—from Frankenstein

the spot. The sky became clouded, but the air was pure, although chilled by the northeast breeze that was then rising. But it refreshed me and filled me with such agreeable sensations that I resolved to prolong my stay on the water, and fixing the rudder in a direct position, stretched myself at the bottom of the boat. Clouds hid the moon, everything was obscure, and I heard only the sound of the boat as its keel cut through the waves; the murmur lulled me, and in a short time I slept soundly.

I do not know how long I remained in this situation, but when I awoke I found that the sun had already mounted considerably. The wind was high, and the waves continually threatened the safety of my little skiff. I found that the wind was northeast and must have driven me far from the coast from which I had embarked. I endeavoured to change my course but quickly found that if I again made the attempt the boat would be instantly filled with water.

Thus situated, my only resource was to drive before the wind. I confess that I felt a few sensations of terror. I had no compass with me and was so slenderly acquainted with the geography of this part of the world that the sun was of little benefit to me. I might be driven into the wide Atlantic and feel all the tortures of starvation or be swallowed up in the immeasurable waters that roared and buffeted around me. I had already been out many hours and felt the torment of a burning thirst, a prelude to my other sufferings. I looked on the heavens, which were covered by clouds that flew before the wind, only to be replaced by others; I looked upon the sea; it was to be my grave. 'Fiend,' I exclaimed, 'your task is already fulfilled!' I

Escape

I am a rudder in rough waves
endeavored to change course
before the waters flood my aim.

—from Frankenstein

Make two poems from the same page,
starting one at the top and one at the bottom.

the spot. The sky became clouded, but the air was pure, although chilled by the northeast breeze that was then rising. But it refreshed me and filled me with such agreeable sensations that I resolved to prolong my stay in the water, and fixing the rudder in a direct position, stretched myself at the bottom of the boat. Clouds hid the moon, everything was obscure, and I heard only the sound of the boat as its keel cut through the waves; the murmur lulled me, and in a short time I sleep soundly.

I do not know how long I remained in this situation, but when I awoke I found that the sun had already mounted considerably. The wind was high, and the waves continually threatened the safety of my little skiff. I found that the wind was northeast and must have driven me far from the coast from which I had embarked. I endeavoured to change my course but quickly found that if I again made the attempt the boat would be instantly filled with water.

Thus situated, my only recourse was to drive before the wind. I confess that I felt a few sensations of terror. I had no compass with me and was so slenderly acquainted with the geography of this part of the world that the sun was of little benefit to me. I might be driving into the wide Atlantic and feel all the tortures of starvation or be swallowed up in the immeasurable waters that roared and buffeted around me. I had already been out many hours and felt the torment of a burning thirst, a prelude to my other sufferings. I looked on the heavens, which were covered by clouds that flew before the wind, only to be replaced by others; I looked upon the sea; it was to be my grave. 'Fiend,' I exclaimed, 'your task is already fulfilled!' I

—*from Frankenstein*

the spot. The sky became clouded, but the air was pure, although chilled by the northeast breeze that was then rising. But it refreshed me and filled me with such agreeable sensations that I resolved to prolong my stay in the water, and fixing the rudder in a direct position, stretched myself at the bottom of the boat. Clouds hid the moon, everything was obscure, and I heard only the sound of the boat as its keel cut through the waves; the murmur lulled me, and in a short time I sleep soundly.

I do not know how long I remained in this situation, but when I awoke I found that the sun had already mounted considerably. The wind was high, and the waves continually threatened the safety of my little skiff. I found that the wind was northeast and must have driven me far from the coast from which I had embarked. I endeavoured to change my course but quickly found that if I again made the attempt the boat would be instantly filled with water.

Thus situated, my only recourse was to drive before the wind. I confess that I felt a few sensations of terror. I had no compass with me and was so slenderly acquainted with the geography of this part of the world that the sun was of little benefit to me. I might be driving into the wide Atlantic and feel all the tortures of starvation or be swallowed up in the immeasurable waters that roared and buffeted around me. I had already been out many hours and felt the torment of a burning thirst, a prelude to my other sufferings. I looked on the heavens, which were covered by clouds that flew before the wind, only to be replaced by others; I looked upon the sea; it was to be my grave. 'Fiend,' I exclaimed, 'your task is already fulfilled!' I

—*from Frankenstein*

Lesson 5:
This Is My Design

Blackout poetry is an art that actively encourages experimentation, taking on numerous forms and aesthetics to convey its personality. From simple crossouts on the page to interactive sculptures, a poet has thousands of design options at their fingertips to both elevate and deepen their piece. A thoughtful design works in tandem with the writing, capable of conjuring feelings of anxiety, nostalgia, eroticism, and more.

However, it's important not to compromise the poem's legibility in service of the design. The design should enhance the reader's experience and the ease at which they absorb the work. After ruminating on a poem's shape and potential art, you might find yourself re-editing during this stage to make the poem flow and/or fit better within the space. For example, if your own option for a word like "the" looks detached from the rest of the poem's body, look for a hidden "the" in a closer word, like in "mother," "anthem" or "feather."

~~Don't~~ Give Me that Tone

Background colors set the mood while the method of connecting your words escorts the reader around the page. The shapes used to outline words, or maybe the lack of, can convey certain emotional weights, and the shape of the poem itself can protect the piece from the distracting unnecessary text. Using pen and paint, thread and tape, glitter and scissors and glue, you can cover superfluous words or remove them entirely, depending on what you believe best represents the poem's theme.

In the following example, I opted to turn the unused portions of the page into a night sky.

I did not fear breaking even

if my confidence proved misplaced. I was

going to cross the

in search of myself.

Observe Again

I did not fear breaking.
Even if my confidence proved misplaced,
I was going to cross the wide brimmed hat of Saturn
In search of myself.

   —*from Wuthering Heights*

Using low-tack tape to protect my chosen words—and some oddly shaped stars—I slathered chalkboard paint over the extra text, leaving only a circle around "wide-brimmed hat of Saturn," to transform into the aforementioned planet. But you might notice that Saturn's rings, as well as the word "Saturn" are on separate pieces of paper. The letters I used to build the word "Saturn" were actually a little further down the line, above the phrase "in search of myself," but since I wanted it to be contained within my little world, I sliced it out and pasted it on a strip of paper I cut from another page of *Wuthering Heights* to make my galactic rings.

Sometimes the poem demands to be heard through papercraft and glitter-glue and bombastic shades of neon. Color-mixing can be an interesting way to set the scene, because you can lean into typical hues to convey certain emotions, or you can seek out new and intriguing ways to convey universal themes. Maybe love isn't red or pink; maybe it's dark brown with the shimmer of moisture, like the deep, fertile earth where we all began…perhaps vines creep out, through the page, sprouting big white blossoms that cradle the words of your poem. Maybe death isn't black, but yellow, like a bruise that never fully heals, haloing the words branded on the flesh of the page.

But sometimes a simple design is best—or something that appears simple, like this design for "The Dragon."

'Why, kiss her awake, of course.'

'Not me!' was Gerald's unhesitating rejoinder.

'Well, someone's got to.'

'She'd go for me as likely as not the minute she woke up,' said Gerald anxiously.

'I'd do it like a shot,' said Kathleen, 'but I don't suppose it 'ud make any difference me kissing her.'

She did it; and it didn't. The Princess still lay in deep slumber.

'Then you must, Jimmy. I dare say you'll do. Jump back quickly before she can hit you.'

'She won't hit him, he's such a little chap,' said Gerald.

'Little yourself!' said Jimmy. '*I* don't mind kissing her. I'm not a coward, like Some People. Only if I do, I'm going to be the dauntless leader for the rest of the day.'

'No, look here – hold on!' cried Gerald, 'perhaps I'd better –' But, in the meantime, Jimmy had planted a loud, cheerful-sounding kiss on the Princess's pale cheek, and now the three stood breathless, awaiting the result.

And the result was that the Princess opened large, dark eyes, stretched out her arms, yawned a little, covering her mouth with a small brown hand, and said, quite plainly and distinctly, and without any room at all for mistake:

'Then the hundred years are over? How the yew hedges have grown! Which of you is my Prince that aroused me from my deep sleep of so many long years?'

'I did,' said Jimmy fearlessly, for she did not look as

The Dragon

The kiss woke her
 But quick to hunger,
The princess opened her mouth
And ate the prince

    —from The Enchanted Castle

Okay, inky cohorts
...are you ready for a BLACKOUT?

'Why, kiss her awake, of course.'

'Not me!' was Gerald's unhesitating rejoinder.

'Well, someone's got to.'

'She'd go for me as likely as not the minute she woke up,' said Gerald anxiously.

'I'd do it like a shot,' said Kathleen, 'but I don't suppose it 'ud make any difference me kissing her.'

She did it; and it didn't. The Princess still lay in deep slumber.

'Then you must, Jimmy. I dare say you'll do. Jump back quickly before she can hit you?'

'She won't hit him, he's such a little chap,' said Gerald.

'Little yourself!' said Jimmy. '*I* don't mind kissing her. I'm not a coward, like Some People. Only if I do, I'm going to be the dauntless leader for the rest of the day.'

'No, look here—hold on!' cried Gerald, 'perhaps I'd better—' But, in the meantime, Jimmy had planted a loud, cheerful-sounding kiss on the Princess's pale cheek, and now the three stood breathless, awaiting the result.

And the result was that the Princess opened large, dark eyes, stretched out her arms, yawned a little, covering her mouth with a small brown hand, and said, quite plainly and distinctly, and without any room at all for mistake:

'Then the hundred years are over? How the yew hedges have grown! Which of you is my Prince that aroused me from my deep sleep of so many long years?'

'I did,' said Jimmy fearlessly, for she did not look as

—*from The Enchanted Castle*

and lock my door?"

She was lying with her tiny hands buried in her rich wavy hair, under her cheek, her little head upon the pillow, and her glittering eyes followed me wherever I moved, with a kind of shy smile that I could not decipher.

I bid her good night, and crept from the room with an uncomfortable sensation.

I often wondered whether our pretty guest ever said her prayers. I certainly had never seen her upon her knees. In the morning she never came down until long after our family prayers were over, and at night she never left the drawing room to attend our brief evening prayers in the hall.

If it had not been that it had casually come out in one of our careless talks that she had been baptised, I should have doubted her being a Christian. Religion was a subject on which I had never heard her speak a word. If I had known the world better, this particular neglect or antipathy would not have so much surprised me.

The precautions of nervous people are infectious, and persons of a like temperament are pretty sure, after a time, to imitate them. I had adopted Carmilla's habit of locking her bedroom door, having taken into my head all her whimsical alarms about midnight invaders and prowling assassins. I had also adopted her precaution of making a brief search through her room, to satisfy herself that no lurking assassin or robber was "ensconced."

These wise measures taken, I got into my bed and fell asleep. A light was burning in my room. This was an old habit, of very early date, and which nothing could have tempted me to dispense

—from Carmilla

Chapter 6

'There was someone crying—there was!'

THE NEXT DAY THE rain poured down in torrents again, and when Mary looked out of her window the moor was almost hidden by grey mist and cloud. There.could be no going out today.

'What do you do in your cottage when it rains like this?' she asked Martha.

'Try to keep from under each other's feet mostly,' Martha answered. 'Eh. there does seem a lot of us then. Mother's a good-tempered woman, but she gets fair moithered. The biggest ones goes out in th' cow-shed and plays there. Dickon he doesn't mind th' wet. He goes out just th' same as if th' sun was shinin'. He says he sees things on rainy days as doesn't show when it's fair weather. He once found a little fox cub half drowned in its hole and he brought it home in th' bosom of his shirt to keep it warm. Its mother had been killed near by an' th' hole was swum out an' th' rest o' th' litter was dead. He's got it at home now. He found a half-drowned young crow another time an' he brought it home, too, an' tamed it. It's named Soot, because it's so black an' it hops an' flies about with him everywhere.'

The time had come when Mary had forgotten to resent Martha's familiar talk. She had even begun to find it interesting and to be sorry when she stopped or went away. The stories she had been told by her Ayah when she lived in India had been quite unlike those Martha had to tell about the moorland cottage which held fourteen people who lived in four little rooms and never had quite enough to eat. The children seemed to tumble about and amuse themselves like a litter of rough, good-natured collie puppies. Mary was most attracted by the mother and Dickon. When Martha told stories of what "mother' said or did they always sounded comfortable.

'If I had a raven or a fox cub I could play with it,' said Mary. 'But I have nothing.

Martha looked perplexed.

"Can tha' knit?' she asked.

—*from The Secret Garden*

the spot. The sky became clouded, but the air was pure, although chilled by the northeast breeze that was then rising. But it refreshed me and filled me with such agreeable sensations that I resolved to prolong my stay in the water, and fixing the rudder in a direct position, stretched myself at the bottom of the boat. Clouds hid the moon, everything was obscure, and I heard only the sound of the boat as its keel cut through the waves; the murmur lulled me, and in a short time I sleep soundly.

I do not know how long I remained in this situation, but when I awoke I found that the sun had already mounted considerably. The wind was high, and the waves continually threatened the safety of my little skiff. I found that the wind was northeast and must have driven me far from the coast from which I had embarked. I endeavoured to change my course but quickly found that if I again made the attempt the boat would be instantly filled with water.

Thus situated, my only recourse was to drive before the wind. I confess that I felt a few sensations of terror. I had no compass with me and was so slenderly acquainted with the geography of this part of the world that the sun was of little benefit to me. I might be driving into the wide Atlantic and feel all the tortures of starvation or be swallowed up in the immeasurable waters that roared and buffeted around me. I had already been out many hours and felt the torment of a burning thirst, a prelude to my other sufferings. I looked on the heavens, which were covered by clouds that flew before the wind, only to be replaced by others; I looked upon the sea; it was to be my grave. 'Fiend,' I exclaimed, 'your task is already fulfilled!' I

—*from Frankenstein*

Congratulations on finding the cheat code section, cleverly hidden behind Lesson 5! Over the last few years studying this art form, I've learned a few tips and tricks that I will happily share with my aspiring blackout artists.

Finding poems

To experiment with potential paths without the risk of erasures, take a picture of the page and work digitally.

Rather than circling/boxing words on the page, use light (parentheses) or straight lines to avoid accidental erasures.

If you know how you'd like your poem to end but can't find the right word, or if building it makes it difficult to read, refer to a thesaurus to find an alternate word.

When looking for a specific word in a book without perusing the entire physical text, search a digital version online. The pages probably won't match up, but it can shorten the process.

Building words

Learn to recognize the words hidden within words. To feminize male-centric passages, look for the "her" hidden in words like "there" and "where" and "other." I'm currently working on a *Wuthering Heights* inspired collection, and I'm very grateful for "Heathcliff." It's given me so much "he," "eat," and "if."

When building a word over multiple lines, look for the least common letter first. Find your X's, K's, V's, etc, and build from there.

Pay attention to suffixes that can be linked with the first letter of the following word to build new ones. For example, the word <u>REST</u> appears three times in the following sentence: We're standing here stoic as wire statues.

We're standing here stoic as wire statues.

Adding Art

Cover your chosen words with low-tack tape (or washi tape) before drawing and painting to protect them while you work through your design.

You can also cover your words with transparent tape (on both sides), paint over everything, and use & alcohol to clean off the paint.

After using watercolor, put a heavy book on top of the page while it dries to minimize wrinkling.

Rubber cement works better on book pages than any other adhesive I've tried.

If you accidentally color over a word and can't salvage it, find the same word in another part of the book (as close to the origin page as possible to ensure the print/paper match the shade) and glue it over the mistake. A thoughtful outline and/or shading can hide the edge.

I nearly titled this closing section "Game Over" but immediately rethought it because your fun is just beginning! Your very own poetic playground awaits, and equipped with these tips and tricks, along with your unmatched artistic instincts, you can trust you're going to create something magical or maniacal, heartbreaking or hilarious, maybe all from the same page and definitely uniquely you.

You'll make mistakes—a lot of them, and forever—but creativity is a faith that loves to forgive, so try to give yourself the same amount of grace, and use your mistakes to learn, grow, and enjoy the mess.

Before I send you on your merry/messy way, I want to thank you all for playing along with me. In these pages, but also for the last several years I've been crafting blackout poems. This artform brought a luster and depth to my writing life that I sorely needed and can never repay. So I'm paying it forward with this playbook in the hope that blackout poetry will nurture your creativity and stretch your imagination like it did for me.

Now, with all my inspirado, I send you into unexplored worlds within worlds, my fellow panners of literary gold and builders of strange hodgepodge nests, to become champions of Seek & Hide.

—Jessica McHugh

Using your new Seek and Hide skills, have
fun making blackout poetry from every
page of your playbook!!

ing on each other, were not interrupted by the casualties that took place around them. The more I saw of them, the greater became my desire to claim their protection and kindness; my heart yearned to be known and loved by these amiable creatures; to see their sweet looks directed towards me with affection was the utmost limit of my ambition. I dared not think that they would turn them from me with disdain and horror. The poor that stopped at their door were never driven away. I asked, it is true, for greater treasures than a little food or rest: I required kindness and sympathy; but I did not believe myself unworthy of it.

'The winter advanced, and an entire revolution of the seasons had taken place since I awoke into life. My attention at this time was solely directed towards my plan of introducing myself into the cottage of my protectors. I revolved many projects, but that on which I finally fixed was to enter the dwelling when the blind old man should be alone. I had sagacity enough to discover that the unnatural hideousness of my person was the chief object of horror with those who had formerly beheld me. My voice, although harsh, had nothing terrible in it; I thought, therefore, that if in the absence of his children I could gain the good will and mediation of the old De Lacey, I might by his means be tolerated by my younger protectors.

'One day, when the sun shone on the red leaves that strewed the ground and diffused cheerfulness, although it denied warmth, Safie, Agatha, and Felix departed on a long country walk, and the old man, at his own desire, was left alone in the cottage. When his children had departed, he took up his guitar and played several mournful but sweet airs, more sweet and mourn-

—from Frankenstein

Act I, Scene 5]

[*Enter Macbeth.*

Great Glamis! worthy Cawdor!
Greater than both, by the all-hail hereafter!
Thy letters have transported me beyond
This ignorant present, and I feel now
The future in the instant.

MACBETH

      My dearest love,
Duncan comes here tonight.

LADY MACBETH

      And when goes hence?
Macbeth
Tomorrow, as he purposes.

LADY MACBETH

      O, never
Shall sun that morrow see!
Your face, my thane, is as a book where men
May read strange matters. To beguile the time,
Look like the time; bear welcome in your eye,
Your hand, your tongue: look like the innocent flower,
But be the serpent under 't. He that's coming
Must be provided for: and you shall put
This night's great business into my dispatch;
Which shall to all our nights and days to come
Give solely sovereign sway and masterdom.

MACBETH
We will speak further.

LADY MACBETH

      Only look up clear;
To alter favor ever is to fear: Leave all the rest to me.

[Exeunt.

—from Macbeth

the petted things, we did despise them! When would you catch me wishing to have what Catherine wanted? or find us by ourselves, seeking entertainment in yelling, and sobbing, and rolling on the ground, divided by the whole room? I'd not exchange, for a thousand lives, my condition here, for Edgar Linton's at Thrushcross Grange—not if I might have the privilege of flinging Joseph off the highest gable, and painting the house-front with Hindley's blood!'

'Hush, hush!' I interrupted. 'Still you have not told me, Heathcliff, how Catherine is left behind?'

'I told you we laughed,' he answered. 'The Lintons heard us, and with one accord, they shot like arrows to the door; there was silence, and then a cry, "Oh, mamma, mamma! Oh, papa! Oh, mamma, come here. Oh, papa, oh!" They really did howl out, something in that way. We made frightful noises to terrify them still more, and then we dropped off the ledge, because somebody was drawing the bars, and we felt we had better flee. I had Cathy by the hand, and was urging her on, when all at once she fell down.

'"Run, Heathcliff, run!" she whispered. "They have let the bulldog loose, and he holds me!"

'The devil had seized her ankle, Nelly; I heard his abominable snorting. She did not yell out—no! She would have scorned to do it, if she had been spitted on the horns of a mad cow. I did, though: I vociferated curses enough to annihilate any fiend in Christendom, and I got a stone and thrust it between his jaws, and tried with all my might to cram it down his throat. A beast of a servant came up with a lantern, at last, shouting—

'"Keep fast, Skulker, keep fast!"

'He changed his note, however, when he saw Skulker's game. The dog was throttled off, his huge, purple tongue hanging half a foot out of his mouth, and his pendant lips streaming with bloody slaver.

'The man took Cathy up; she was sick; not from fear, I'm certain, but from pain. He carried her in; I followed, grumbling execrations and vengeance.

—*from Wuthering Heights*

terms in which he expressed himself.

"I should tell you all with pleasure," said the General, "but you would not believe me."

"Why should I not?" he asked.

"Because," he answered testily, "you believe in nothing but what consists with your own prejudices and illusions. I remember when I was like you, but I have learned better."

"Try me," said my father; "I am not such a dogmatist as you suppose.

Besides which, I very well know that you generally require proof for what you believe, and am, therefore, very strongly predisposed to respect your conclusions."

"You are right in supposing that I have not been led lightly into a belief in the marvelous for what I have experienced is marvelous and I have been forced by extraordinary evidence to credit that which ran counter, diametrically, to all my theories. I have been made the dupe of a preternatural conspiracy."

Notwithstanding his professions of confidence in the General's penetration, I saw my father, at this point, glance at the General, with, as I thought, a marked suspicion of his sanity.

The General did not see it, luckily. He was looking gloomily and curiously into the glades and vistas of the woods that were opening before us.

"You are going to the Ruins of Karnstein?" he said. "Yes, it is a lucky coincidence; do you know I was going to ask you to bring me there to inspect them. I have a special object in exploring. There is a ruined chapel, ain't there, with a great many tombs of that extinct family?"

—from Carmilla

Jessica McHugh

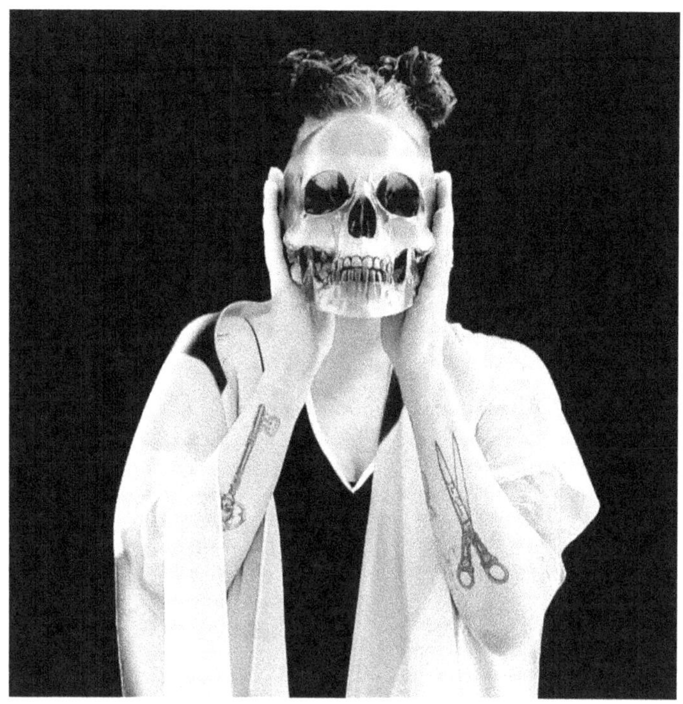

Jessica McHugh is a 3x Bram Stoker Award-nominated poet, a multi-genre novelist, & an internationally-produced playwright who spends her days surrounded by artistic inspiration at a Maryland tattoo shop. She's had thirty books published in fifteen years, including her Elgin Award-nominated blackout poetry collection, *The Quiet Ways I Destroy You*, her sci-fi bizarro romp, *The Green Kangaroos*, and her cross-generational horror series, *The Gardening Guidebooks Trilogy*. Explore the growing worlds of Jessica McHugh at McHughniverse.com.

Bibliography

- Carmilla - Sheridan Le Fanu

- Dracula - Bram Stoker

- The Enchanted Castle - Edith Nesbit

- Frankenstein - Mary Shelley

- MacBeth - William Shakespeare

- The Secret Garden - Frances Hodgson Burnett

- Wuthering Heights - Emily Bronte

Pen Test!

Use this space to test your pens, markers and writing implements for color, bleed or just to see if they are actually still working

Pen Test!

www.ingramcontent.com/pod-product-compliance
Lightning Source LLC
Chambersburg PA
CBHW080837160726
47999CB00009B/2920